P9-DXC-529

Giggle Fit®
crazy christmas Jokes

Alison Grambs

Illustrated by
Steve Harpster

Sterling Publishing Co., Inc.
New York

Library of Congress Cataloging-in-Publication Data

10 9 8 7 6 5 4 3 2 1

Published by Sterling Publishing Co., Inc.
387 Park Avenue South, New York, NY 10016
© 2004 by Alison Grambs
Distributed in Canada by Sterling Publishing
^{c}/o Canadian Manda Group, One Atlantic Avenue, Suite 105
Toronto, Ontario, Canada M6K 3E7
Distributed in Great Britain and Europe by Chris Lloyd at Orca Book
Services, Stanley House, Fleets Lane, Poole BH15 3AJ, England
Distributed in Australia by Capricorn Link (Australia) Pty. Ltd.
P.O. Box 704, Windsor, NSW 2756, Australia

Sterling ISBN 1-4027-1244-8

Knock-Knock.
  Who's there?
Sandy.
  Sandy who?
Sandy Claus is coming to town.

Knock-Knock.
  Who's there?
Water.
  Water who?
Water you asking Santa for this year?

Is Santa's toy shop open all year?

No, it's usually Claus-ed until December.

What did Santa say when he got back to the North Pole?

"There's snow place like home."

Knock-Knock.

Who's there?

Ivana.

Ivana who?

Ivana sit on Santa's lap next!

What breed of dog guards Santa's workshop?

The toy poodle.

How do you get Santa's attention when he's flying his sled in a snowstorm?
You hail him.

Why is Santa looking for a new job?
Because he got sacked.

Knock-Knock.
Who's there?
Coal.
Coal who?
Coal me if you hear Santa is coming.

What happened when Santa
parked his sled illegally?
He got mistle-towed.

What song does Santa sing?
**"You beard-er watch out,
you beard-er not cry."**

Why did Santa get a ticket
on Christmas Eve?
**He left his sled in a
"Snow Parking Zone."**

Why was the manger so crowded on Christmas Eve?
Because the Three Wide Men showed up.

Knock-Knock.
Who's there?
Tree.
Tree who?
Tree wise men, silly!

Where do the Three Wise Men get their robes shortened?
Bethle-hem.

Did Mrs. Claus have to serve Santa's helpers dinner?
No, they helped them-elves to it!

How did Mrs. Claus know her husband wanted a new bicycle for Christmas?
Because he spoke about it a lot.

SANTA CLAUS: Have you seen Rudolph? I can't find him anywhere!
MRS. CLAUS: He's right over deer playing with the elves.

How does Mrs. Claus help Santa?
She pays all the jingle bills.

Do female reindeer like Mrs. Claus?
Yes, they fawn all over her.

Why does Rudolph do well at trivia games?
Because he nose a lot.

Why is Rudolph seen at the public library a lot?
Because he's very well-red.

Knock-Knock.
Who's there?
Annie.
Annie who?
Annie one see Rudolph yet?

How does Rudolph address a letter to his boss?
"Deer Santa."

Knock-Knock.
Who's there?
Anita.
Anita who?
Anita lift, Rudolph. Can you give me one?

What does Santa find most annoying about Rudolph?
He's always fa-la-la-la-la-lowing him around.

What vacuum does Rudolph use?
A Hoofer.

What does Santa get on his suit when he ice skates?
Rink around the collar.

Where does Santa hang his red suit?
In the Claus-et.

Why was Frosty the Snowman wearing a sweater?
Because it was coal-ed outside.

How can you tell if a Christmas tree is female?
It's wearing a tree skirt.

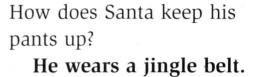

How does Santa keep his pants up?

He wears a jingle belt.

What version of "Silent Night" do socks sing?

"Silent Night, Holey Night."

Why didn't the Christmas stockings finish their dinner?

Because they were stuffed.

What baseball position do elves play?
Shortstop.

Knock-Knock.
Who's there?
Elf.
Elf who?
Elf I knock again, will you let me in?

Why was Santa's helper so shy?
Because he had no elf-confidence.

Is making Christmas toys difficult?
No, it just takes a little elf-ort.

What kind of seafood
do elves love?
Shrimp.

What is Santa's
favorite animal?
An elfant.

15

What is Santa's favorite basketball team?
The New York Old St. Knicks.

What do golfers eat on the course?
Plum putt-ing.

What do baseball players serve on Christmas?
Bunt cake.

What position does the Christmas turkey play in the World Series?
First baste.

What do you decorate a gym with at Christmas?
Muscle-toe.

What do golfers decorate their home with for the holidays?
Christmas tees.

What do baseball batters do for Christmas?
Swing Christmas carols.

How does a Christmas tree freshen its breath?

It eats an orna-mint.

What do you call a Christmas tree with a big nose?

Pine-nocchio.

What do geometrists place on the very top of their Christmas trees?

Angles.

Why did the Christmas tree lose on the game show?
The final question stumped it.

Are Christmas trees risk takers?
Yes, they go out on a limb.

Where do they make movies about famous Christmas trees?
In Tinsel Town.

Do Christmas trees knit?
No, they do needle-point.

How do you greet the U.S. President during a Christmas blizzard?
"Hail to the Chief."

Why can't you rely on snow?
It can be a bit flakey.

Knock-Knock.
Who's there?
Sink.
Sink who?
Sink it'll snow on Christmas this year?

Where did Mrs. Frosty meet Mr. Frosty?

At the Snow Ball.

What aisle at the grocery store does Frosty the Snowman love?

The frozen food section.

What sandwich scares Frosty the Snowman?

A tuna melt.

What holiday drink really gets on your nerves?
Eggnag.

What's a really gross Christmas drink?
Ick nog.

On what holiday did the ham get burnt?
On Crispmas Eve.

Why doesn't Santa like shellfish?
It makes him crabby.

What do salads wish for at Christmas?
Peas on Earth and goodwill toward men.

What do Canadians serve for
dessert on Christmas Eve?
Chocolate moose.

What kind of gifts
does a baker get for
Christmas?
Crumby ones.

Knock-Knock.
Who's there?
Ham.
Ham who?
**Ham I going to get everything
I asked for this year, Santa?**

Knock-Knock.
Who's there?
Gift.
Gift who?
**Gift me a piece of that
fruitcake, will you?**

How do computers like their Christmas cookies?
In byte-size pieces.

How do buffalo like their
Christmas dinners?
On the plain side.

Knock-Knock.

Who's there?

Pudding.

Pudding who?

Pudding the ribbon on Christmas presents is the most important part.

Knock-Knock.

Who's there?

Cashew.

Cashew who?

Cashew peeking at the presents and you'll be in big trouble!

What's Santa's favorite sandwich?

Peanut butter and jolly.

Why do fish love Christmas?
Because they don't have to go to school for the whole week.

How did Santa feel when he forgot to bring his pet fish a present?
Gill-ty.

What do fish decorate their trees with on Christmas?
Fin-sel.

How do fish celebrate
Christmas?
**By hanging
holiday reefs on
the door.**

What do you call a
blizzard of fish?
Snow flukes.

How do fish learn to play
Christmas carols on the piano?
By practicing their scales.

Do fish like holiday fruitcake?
Yes, they're totally hooked on it!

Why did Santa start sneezing
in the chimney?
He caught a nasty floo.

Why can't Santa
ride horses?
**He gets real bad
hay fever.**

Why did the Christmas tree lights go
to the eye doctor?
Because they were on the blink.

Who cut himself shaving on Christmas?
Old St. Nick.

What sound does Santa make when he sneezes in a chimney?
Ash-hoooo!

How does Santa scratch an itch?
With his Claus.

How did Santa walk when he sprained his ankle?
With a candy cane.

Why is Christmas a good time to buy a boat?
Because they're on sail.

What do sailors put on ships during the holidays?
Deck-orations.

How do you decorate a canoe for Christmas?
With oar-naments.

Why do Christmas trees always cry at sad movies?

Because they're real saps.

Why was Santa crying?

He Mrs. Claus.

Why was the Christmas tree crying?

Because he was pining away for his mommy.

Why was the little squirrel upset with Santa?

Because he got nut-in' good in his Christmas stocking.

How did Santa get lost on Christmas Eve?
He got mis-sled.

How did Santa get back to the North Pole?
He drove all the sleigh home.

Knock-Knock.
  Who's there?
Needle.
  Needle who?
Needle lift to the North Pole, Santa?

DASHER: Hey, what's that reindeer doing with Santa's sled?
RUDOLPH: He's just Vixen the broken engine.

How did the Christmas angel get to the North Pole?
  She winged it.

What did Santa bring the bear for Christmas?
  A cub-vertible car.

BEAR #1: Is Santa Claus coming to town?

BEAR #2: Yes, I'm absolutely paws-itive he'll be here.

What does a grizzly bear's Christmas tree look like?
It is decorated with grrrrr-land.

Where do bears celebrate Christmas with their families?
In log cub-bins.

What can pigs always be found doing on Christmas Eve?
Bacon cookies for Santa Claus.

Where can a pig find Santa Claus?
At the Snort Pole.

Why are pigs annoying on Christmas?
Because they're always hogging the presents.

Why does Santa get a lot of laughs at Christmas dinner?
Because he's such a ham.

Why was the fruitcake acting so silly at school?
It was in a real nutty mood.

Why are Christmas packages so easy to make fun of?
Because they take a lot of ribbon.

How did Santa do at the comedy club?
Oh, he sleighed them!

Knock-Knock.
   Who's there?
Yuletide.
   Yuletide who?
**Yuletide yourself over
with a snack until dinner.**

Why was the chimney
looking for a new job?
   Because it got fired.

Why did the chimney
write a letter to Santa?
   **It wanted to ash for
   a new bicycle.**

Knock-Knock.
  Who's there?
Art.
  Art who?
Art you coming Christmas caroling with us?

What Christmas carol do dogs sing?
  "Deck the howls with bows of holly."

What song do elephants like to sing on the holidays?
"I'm dreaming of a wide Christmas."

What do you call singing horses?
Christmas Corral-ers.

What's the chorus to a goblin's favorite Christmas song?
Troll-la-la-la-la-la-la-la-la.

What instruments do reindeer play in the orchestra?
Horns.

What's very popular on the radio at Christmas time?
Wrap music.

What Christmas gifts are hard to get rid of?
Sticking stuffers.

What did Santa get the chicken for Christmas?
An alarm cluck.

How does Santa decide which sailors get Christmas presents?
He asks them who's been knotty and who's been nice.

Who brings Christmas
gifts to lobsters?
Santa Claws.

Who brings Christmas gifts to fleas?
Old St. Tick.

When do tired kids open
their presents?
**On Christmas
yawning.**

Did the baby cow like
his Christmas gifts?
**Yes, he was udderly
thrilled.**

Why is the Christmas present in honors class?
Because it is a gift-ed student.

Knock-Knock.
Who's there?
Christmas.
Christmas who?
Christmas be at school by 9 AM or his teacher will count him as absent.

What's Santa's least favorite part about school?
Doing his ho-ho-homework.

Where do Christmas trees go to borrow books?
The nearest library branch.

DASHER: Where are you spending the holidays this year?

DANCER: I'm having Christmas dinner at my uncle and aunt-ler's house.

Why are reindeer popular at campfires?

Because they tell good tails.

What kind of deer carry umbrellas?

Rain-deer.

Who is the fastest reindeer?

Dasher.

What did the Headless Horseman get for Christmas?
A really nice necktie.

What gift does Santa give to ghosts?
Cookbooooks.

What do witches ring on Christmas Day?
Jinxle bells.

Who's worth about five cents at Christmas time?
Old St. Nickel.

Are Christmas trees expensive?
No, their prices are very wreath-onable.

Did Santa's elves have enough money to buy him a gift?
No, they fell a little short this year.

What do puppies put on their Christmas trees?
Candy cane-ines.

Why don't cats like Christmas shopping?
They can't stand waiting in felines.

Why do sharks love Santa Claus so much?
Because he's a jaw-ly good fellow!

What does Santa's dog wear to keep warm in the North Pole?
Earmutts.

What's a snake's
favorite holiday?
Chrissssssmas.

How does Santa bring toys
to all the little elephants?
In a trunk.

Who's joining the horses for some
Christmas caroling this year?
The nay-bors.

INDEX